Safe Kids
Water Safety

Dana Meachen Rau

Marshall Cavendish
Benchmark
New York

Splash!

Water feels good on a hot day.

You need to be safe
in water.

A grown-up should
always be with you.

Swim where you can stand.

Do not go too deep.

Swim near a *lifeguard*.

Lifeguards keep swimmers safe.

Always swim with a buddy.

A buddy can call for help.

Never push someone in or under the water.

Never play rough in water.

Do not dive in *shallow* water.

You could hit your head on the bottom.

Watch for other swimmers when you jump.

You could hit someone in a crowded pool.

Beaches can have strong *waves*.

Waves can pull you under or out to sea.

Blow-up toys are fun in water.

But they do not keep you safe.

Only a *life jacket* keeps you safe.

Always wear one in a boat.

Get out of the water if there is a storm.

Lightning can hurt you in the water.

Be a safe kid in water.

Be Safe

buddy

life jacket

lifeguard

pool

28

storm

waves

Challenge Words

lifeguard (LIFE-gard) A person who keeps swimmers safe.

life jacket A vest that helps people float.

shallow (SHAL-oh) Not deep.

waves Bumps of moving water.

Index

Page numbers in **boldface** are illustrations.

About the Author

Dana Meachen Rau is the author of many other titles in the Bookworms series, as well as other nonfiction and early reader books. She lives in Burlington, Connecticut, with her husband and two children.

With thanks to the Reading Consultants:

Nanci Vargus, Ed.D., is an Assistant Professor of Elementary Education at the University of Indianapolis.

Beth Walker Gambro is an Adjunct Professor at the University of Saint Francis in Joliet, Illinois.

Marshall Cavendish Benchmark
99 White Plains Road
Tarrytown, New York 10591-9001
www.marshallcavendish.us

Text copyright © 2010 by Marshall Cavendish Corporation

Library of Congress Cataloging-in-Publication Data

Rau, Dana Meachen, 1971-
Water safety / by Dana Meachen Rau.
p. cm. — (Bookworms: Safe kids)
Includes index.
Summary: "Identifies common water hazards and advises how to deal with them"
—Provided by publisher.
ISBN 978-0-7614-4088-8
1. Aquatic sports—Safety measures—Juvenile literature. I. Title.
GV770.6.R375 2010
797.20028'9—dc22
2008044930

Editor: Christina Gardeski
Publisher: Michelle Bisson
Designer: Virginia Pope
Art Director: Anahid Hamparian

Photo Research by Anne Burns Images

Cover Photo by *Alamy Images*/Chuck Franklin

The photographs in this book are used with permission and through the courtesy of:
Corbis: pp. 1, 11, 28TL Fabio Cardoso/zefa; p. 3 Kiyotaka Kitajima; pp. 19, 29R Flynn Larsen/zefa;
pp. 23, 28TR Tony Demin; pp. 25, 29L Jim Reed.
Alamy Images: p. 5 Craig Lovell/Eagle Visions Photography; p. 7 Ben Ramos.
SuperStock: pp. 9, 28BL age fotostock. *Getty*: pp. 13, 27 Dorgie Productions;
p. 15 Grant Symon; p. 17, 28BR Joos Mind; p. 21 Gary Chapman.

Printed in Malaysia
1 3 5 6 4 2

E 9/12

R

(yellow)